D0283756

DENIABILITY

Also by GEORGE WITTE

The Apparitioners

DENIABILITY

GEORGE WITTE

ORCHISES
WASHINGTON
2009

EASTERN SHORE PUBLIC LIBRARY
Accomac, Virginia 23301

Copyright © 2008 George Witte

Library of Congress Cataloging-in-Publication Data

Witte, George
Deniability / George Witte.
    p. cm.
    ISBN 978-1-932535-19-8 (alk. paper)
    I. Title.
    PS3623.I879D46 2009
    811'.6—dc22

                                    2008030608

ACKNOWLEDGMENTS

Thanks to the editors of these journals for first publishing certain poems in this collection:

Boulevard: "Deniability," "Next," "Person of Interest"

The Kean Review: "Ends or Means," "For the Purposes of This Discussion," "High Command," "I Know an Old Lady," "If You See Something, Say Something," "Master Plan," "Rendition," "Watch List"

New Haven Review: "Failure to Comply," "Friendly Fire," "Hearts and Minds," "The Hero," "Uh-Oh," "You Break It, You Bought It"

New York Quarterly: "We Regret to Inform You"

Prairie Schooner: "Soft Targets," "The Third Pig," "The Ticket"

Shenandoah: "Haptic," "Likenesses"

Smartish Pace: "The Foggiest Notion"

Southwest Review: "A Sudden Loss of Cabin Pressure"

Vocabula: "Hide and Seek," "Turn"

Manufactured in the United States of America

ORCHISES PRESS
P. O. Box 320533
Alexandria
Virginia
22320-4533

G 6 E 4 C 2 A

DENIABILITY

CONTENTS

I

Uh-oh   13

For the Purposes of This Discussion   15

Haptic   16

The Revellers   18

Sunday Morning Hangover   19

Elsewhere   22

The System Crashes   23

Classical Subjects   25

Change   28

How to Survive the Coming   30

The Foggiest Notion   32

The Ticket   33

II

Next   37

High Command   38

Hearts and Minds   39

Master Plan   40

I Know an Old Lady   41

Rendition   42

Just Cause   44

Simultaneous Submission   45

Friendly Fire   47

We Regret to Inform You   48

You Break It, You Bought It   50

Ends or Means   51

Occupation   52

Surge   53

The Hero   55

Deniability   58

III

TURN   63

THE THIRD PIG   64

A SUDDEN LOSS OF CABIN PRESSURE   66

PERSON OF INTEREST   67

TEST   69

SUSPICIOUS ACTS   71

HIDE AND SEEK   73

PAGING   74

NIGHTMARE SCENARIO   75

PAY NO ATTENTION TO THAT MAN BEHIND THE CURTAIN   76

IF YOU SEE SOMETHING, SAY SOMETHING   78

TRIDENT   80

WATCH LIST   82

NINE-TENTHS OF THE LAW   83

NO BRAINER   85

FAILURE TO COMPLY   86

LIKENESSES   88

SOFT TARGETS   89

History doesn't repeat itself, but sometimes it rhymes.

—attributed (falsely) to Mark Twain

I

Uh-Oh

No photograph records
that day's unmaking roar.

Things ripped from skins,
words from definitions.

Letters distilled until
incomprehensible,

whistles, clicks, thrummed diphthongs
an underwater song

too deep for human ears.
We wept, or cursed in fear,

beseeched unanswered phones
Please God, alone,

walked home in single file.
The broken and defiled

crept close within our space,
affording grace

we disregarded, lost:
two beams a blackened cross,

missing person fliers,
watch warped by fire.

No explanation why;
the perfect alibi

your word, no witnesses.
You saw this coming, yes?

Our brazen structures razed,
immense collapse the praise

you craved, that roar's
descending, perfect chord.

FOR THE PURPOSES OF THIS DISCUSSION

Assume one flight is grounded for repair,
details unavailable at this time,
the second changes scheduled gate without
announcing where to run so passengers
stare rapt before the information board
awaiting word, the missing number's glare,
raw weather runway-strands the third for hours
while salesmen access and delete email,
kids fidget, moms explain, dads nap between
corrections issued in the captain's drawl,
free drinks are served with brisk apology
to no avail, another instance where
the system's inefficiencies conspire
against all plans, benevolent or dire,
therefore that morning's overbooking culls
those late arriving passengers who fail
to check in with the gate, so forfeit seats,
are rendered mute with rage and impotent
before procedure, watching as the fourth
backs ungainly out, lumbering through its turn
within fluorescent gesturing of wands,
prepares for takeoff and begins to rev,
accelerates, then lifts into calm air,
flying by instruments and unaware.

HAPTIC

A touch—you turn, too late to greet it—
brings back the year when such
were commonplace, or said to be.
Who knew? If you heeded newsboys
robed in ulsters, Cassandran,
then you believed apocalypse
a nudge away, the world
one nickel's worth of mineral
from eternity, and this extra sense
a sign or summons from the dead come back
to mock their jailers into panic.

If not—you cleaved to hope, and flourished—
then all went on. Through slush,
through silver sun, the city
turning on itself in stalled ballet
no traffic cop could choreograph,
you walked to work. The touches spread
from one to one like ripples in a pond
flooding avenues with portent
and still you walked, or waded rather,
waiting for the day
when you would whirl, bewildered and afraid.

It comes—you turn, too late to greet
or fend it off—but nothing happens:
no gun, no wizened nightmare twin
clawing to your back. Every corner
seems another threshold, as though
you carry something delicate
from block to block toward home,
a bride perhaps, or prayer answered,
or long forgotten promise now fulfilled.
That year comes true;
you feel the world hang fire, and hold.

The Revellers

A man sucks tokens from the turnstile slot
he paper-stuffed, so desperate his kiss
amuses us, commuters rubbernecking
at the wreck. He's contrived a shtick to ease
our souls, each thin coin clenched between chafed lips,
thin arms a tattooed presidential V.
Some spare him a buck to pass, Charon's tip,
admission fee the underworld requires.
The subway roars approach, shoving black air
down our throats. A woman's scream cuts short.
Plugging ears, squinting tight against the grit
I see a flash and flinch as if from gunshot—
some foreign tourist's instant camera
dangles evidence like a tongue stuck out,
developing before our eyes: the train's
cold blur-lit head entering the station,
pale figures turning toward it or away,
hands clasped to heads, bodies hunched, faces drawn
with fear, and in the foreground's focus one
of us not unlike us displays his skill.
His flock laughs wildly, at the edge of rage.
He bends again to mouth the metal nipple.

SUNDAY MORNING HANGOVER

Grilled meat and pissed-out wine's iridescence
sear tongue and eye, morning after ruins
feast for resurrection. The risen sun's
a nightmare of reflected glare from four
directions: scouring shade from doors and over-
hangs it rouses sleepers like a beat cop—
Move along, now—so they do, wander up
8th Avenue to Port Authority
for a cigarette, a leak, some coffee.

But nothing's open: not the pizza guy
from Pakistan who'll sometimes lend a slice,
No pay, no pay, and the China Deli's
ALL DAY 7 DAY blinking light is still.
The city's barren as a winter field.
To strive, to seek, to find, and not to yield—
but what if you can't find? Go figure that.
A beaten army leaves its cardboard-built
encampments to the pigeons, dogs, and rats.

How did you progress (desert's more like it)
from there to here?—top floor above a bar,
stairs blacked out except the fire code Exit.
Shower, shave, and pull your shit together.

You lift the blind, cry out like a vampire.
Hard light carves an edge on the hangover,
hones it to a blade behind your forehead.
You can't remember what you did last night.
You don't watch out one day you'll wake up dead.

A wind picks up, intersects another
so a turn begins, climbing as it spins
outside the window where you sip a beer,
tornado lifting litter into dance:
hot dog wraps, the daily headline horror,
flyers seeking vanished children's effects,
circulars for camera film and LIVE SEXXX,
ash from cigarettes suckled down to black.
The whirling cone glides west on 34th,

where the raging prophet's board claims Earthquake
Soon, Repent Before It's Too Late. For what?
The coming extirpation of the Jews?
Christ in the kaleidoscope of refuse?
Then you'd have it made—camera crews,
the news recited as if holy writ,
suburb pilgrims who'd buy a piece of it
for proof or joke, a grotesque souvenir,
sooty fingernail or hair to show the folks.

God's recombined from predator to pet,
there when he's wanted, locked away when not.

Athletes endorse him like a vitamin;
CEOs put him on their bottom line
in case ambitious shareholders revolt.
Good for what ails you—cancers of the soul
or salary—his word's our wishing well,
a bank eternal where our pennies tossed
compound tax-free, no matter what the cost.

The wind subsides, no miracle today.
The apparition topples. Undercut,
its shabby raiment rains on passersby
who duck and curse the merciless debris.
The sun is fixed like some kid's lens on ants;
scurrying to find shade, they pause, then can't.
Below your window, one guy tries to raise
a buddy who has fallen in the heat
or sleeps it off, dreaming of cool kisses—

No telling which. *Get up. Hey, you okay?*
He squats to check, his face an inch away
where breath could touch if breath were mutual.
He tries to lift against the building wall,
just wedges up the other by degree…
begins to weep, shaking his familiar
stranger, stands back to kick and kick and pray:
Get up already, quit fucking with me.
Jesus Christ I can't take it anymore.

ELSEWHERE

As if blind, each day you navigate
by stars fixed in the mind's eye's midnight.
The path to work deepens from routine—
its level plains and thresholds, crossings
over, potholes that demand a dance
you execute—but elsewhere the plan's
uncharted, monster-ruled and whirlpooled.
Here one false step opens the abyss.
Slipping through your pocket hole a dime
appeases gods you don't give a damn
about. Scylla's a whore, Charybdis
the ruined men who squeegee windshields
for a tip, door of burned-out nightclub
grave from which you hear the lost cry *Fire*,
pounding at the exit. You walk sure-
footed as a mule along the curb
edges of doubt, never looking down.

The System Crashes

A virus infiltrates; disguised
as resumé or compliment
evades IT and subdivides

seeding email with attachments
that when clicked transmit contagion.
Hunched in cubicles, we repent

our sins and curse, minor demons
unyoked from large intelligence,
terrified we'll be abandoned

to our thoughts, the system's silence
like a parent's disapproval.
We pound keys, demanding entrance,

as if that alphabet might spell
some code to reconnect and free
us with the easeful chime of mail.

It's killing productivity;
forbidden cigarettes are used.
Without the web's authority

we buzz like unhived bees, confused.
A few get through on cells to know
what's happened, strobe-illumined news

shifting between light and shadow,
chaotic rumors of attack.
Emerging in the street below

we orient toward home and walk,
squinting in the glare, revenants
from other lives, no looking back.

CLASSICAL SUBJECTS

In the painting, Apollo flays
the beast that challenged his divine
supremacy of song. Bright-eyed
as a child, curious to know,
he peels back flaps of skin. Each cut's
calculated, screams extracted
like purest harp notes, lines of verse
in every fresh incision.
Delicate but firm, his pale hands
play upon the hairy body
swart with dirt, disagreeable,
miscast at foot and ear, brow lined
with origins still unrefined.
He would gladly heal this creature
if surgery cured presumption,
remove whatever gland or lobe
aspired beyond its rightful sphere.
His technique is impeccable.
His instrument glitters with fire.
A crowd has gathered to admire
his work, enlightened by a guide.
Notice the cunning little cat
to lap the blood—an artist's touch.
Behind the tree that binds the beast

(impastoed bark so thick its grain
seems real), rich Tuscan land recedes,
an exercise in perspective.
The god pauses. His masterpiece
might require another brush stroke.
He stays the sun for better light.
These things take time if they're to last.

*

It wasn't what you people think.
The pictures made us animals,
our tongues protruding red and slick,
eyes too, like they'd been fingernailed.
You can't imagine what it's like,
I've never felt so in control,
so free, outside myself but there,
invisible, the camera
my magic shield or spy's disguise.
Things got out of hand, whatever—
some itch that didn't satisfy.
We stripped and hosed the terrorists,
positioned them curled sixty nine,
you know the drill. We trained the dogs
to ask the whereabouts of _____:
that name they fear and won't reveal,
like God's. No names for anything.

We were following procedure.
When you're starved for information
even screaming sounds like music.

*

In the city's underlayer
I planned this poem like a brief,
collecting evidence against
humanity's inheritance.
My thinking was distracted when
a beggar on the subway car
announced his plight in quiet song.
(*Why can't he get a job?* one said.)
He walked the aisle; all watched but none
acknowledged him. In front of me—
beneath my notebook's tidy lines
his feet were flayed—he paused: *Yo, chief.*
I wouldn't look. He touched my arm,
a violation. Summoning
my coldest gaze, superior
with intellect, I met his eyes:
all blood and mucous, the body's
last-ditch desperate remedies.
I don't know what he saw in mine.
He shuffled on. My poem lost,
I cursed his touch until my stop.

CHANGE

Money's time, but no one has it.
A quarter costs your dignity.
Ask for time and they give it free,
precise to the minute,
as if they're late to catch a train.
To live you want to entertain,
play clever rogue or desperate
case—nothing in between.
You have to promise something rich and strange.
Spare a little change and you luck may change.

They cross the street to get away,
or shrug elaborate, then smile
too wide, a simile
of fear contrived to tell me Stay,
like I'm some dog. Bayed animal,
I howl and bark, make fingers claws,
my face a ritual
mask—anything to give them pause
about our common personality.
Spare a little change and you wish may be.

Your do-good prayers aren't worth my time.
You want God, go rub a bottle,

see what starved ghost endures to dwell.
Your favorite son has come
to pay his father's debts, trouble
doubled back on its creator,
the lonely monster stumbling home
to burn—high theater.
You can't escape the children you derange.
Spare a little change and you luck may change.

How to Survive the Coming

TV ads yell Hurry, time's running out.
We shuffle faiths like cards to soothe our doubt.

Lengthen maturity and seek total return.

Extra syllables lend wit to nonsense;
Perhaps they raise investor confidence.

Limit losses and profits will follow the curve.

Years of drought end in flood, God run amok.
News anchor laughs at the weatherman's joke.

Equal dollar weight and leverage your positions.

Woman Made Pregnant With Alien Child.
Husband denies it; the Pope's reconciled.

Consolidation more important than ever.

Energies diminish: our clocks go bust,
Everyone's tired by some mystery virus.

Reinvestment risk is most likely to emerge.

Quiz show contestants argue the problem:
A stone rolled back from which lone gunman's tomb?

Lengthen maturity and seek total return.

The Foggiest Notion

Twenty feet are visible and still
green hills come to mind, peripheral
glimpses that turn your head around.
When we rode to war each stone
rang out its name: *obsidian, granite!*
We were right. The king's sword swung in the sunlight.
Surveying the domain: the ridge
whose trees we'd mapped and blazed,
swell beyond swell to the glittering sea and all
the grass in the world blowing our way—

Well. These moments when your neck
most painfully cricks
and catches as, stumbling through fog,
you look back for landmarks;
when your lead-lined overcoat most
weighs, as before you looms
the ruined city, flooded cellars brackish
graves for rats—these moments
a leaf etched out in frost
(the small near things are friendliest)
leaps to nip your wrist, whispering that
nothing is easy, when it's all there is.

THE TICKET

Beneath the doctor's hammer
Knee can flinch, blood purr warm through veins,
Eyes contract against bright light
And widen through the evenings—

Yet still be dead, the body's
Reflexive dumb machinery
Chattering like a cash box gone awry
While soul slips quietly out,

Pristine white receipt.
Tear it loose the wind will catch it
In an updraft past the tree line of a peak
And—years later, cool ghostly ticket—

Slip it in your hand, Commuter.
You clutch it like a lifeline
Through the city's flotsam,
In the tattooed N or R train

Eeling underground, between stone lions
And a block of airborne litter whirling,

Past the lost whose pure high songs
Suck you near to disappear....

Bewildered in an elevator,
Head bowed before the candid numbers,
You hold your ticket to their light
Squinting for a clue, and wonder

Who the thousand voices were,
What mystery was given you to bear,
When did you depart, and where arrive
With this burning flag before you, naked and alive?

II

NEXT

By popular demand, dictators flee
aboard private plane, cower into holes
from which they're yanked in hirsute infancy
and whisked away, location undisclosed.
Our asset's now a liability
requiring diplomatic solution:
exile, jail, or roadside execution.

We bed these courtesans to foreign aid,
monitor elections, then stabilize,
inspect, affirm, renew embargoed trade.
Democracy entails some compromise;
torture slick with oil, fruit for nothing said
when people disappear. Good government
ensures taxpayer money's wisely spent.

Things come apart, as all arrangements will,
lame recognition that enough's enough—
mass graves unearthed, table scraps of evil.
We're shamed to alter policy or bluff
our hand, ulteriors deniable,
then float the balance of our fathers' dream
to arm and constitute the next regime.

HIGH COMMAND

Bring me the head of that fugitive god,
Mottled and burnt, unmistakably his.
Grasp woven hair as he brandished others',
Example to quell insurgency's hiss.

Last seen ascending impassable peaks,
Whispered alive within border terrain
Where witnesses swear he walks undisguised,
Alias common, indigenous name

Slipping like virus into our software.
Bring me his balls, swart morsels of hide, sun-
Dried in savory strips of their savior,
Gristle and tallow, the host genuine.

Absence made present, belief's bonafides,
Proof special forces extracted like teeth,
Captured, mistaken, confirmed then denied,
Fingerprints lifted from safe houses' walls

Imperfectly matched, anonymous whorls
Feeling for exit from rooms damp with blood.
We no longer know half-truths from the whole.
Bring me the head of that fugitive god.

Hearts and Minds

The heart recoils where mind's inclined
To justify as war expense.
Smells the euphemizing liar's
Sweat condense, penetrate, and dry
Beneath crisp uniform and tie
In rings no cleanser can erase.
Denies the truth when truth's denied,
Withholds opinion pending facts
Revealed irrelevant by faith:
All damage is collateral,
Intelligence reliable,
Election verifiable,
Our casualties acceptable.
The heart believes where mind relies
On evidence from satellites,
Translated cellphone intercepts,
Raw film one cringes to behold
With eyes askance yet curious,
Passerby become apostle
Having witnessed demonstration,
Persuaded not by risen life
But murder's power to appall
The silent heart and free the mind
To contemplate its purposes.

MASTER PLAN

Shock and awe gave way to afterthought,
The unforeseen to revelation's
Flash: enshadowed space where victors strut
Red-eyed, like crows on carrion.

We bomb to lay a righteous cornerstone,
Elect to buy, occupy to free.
Each flea finds blood-warm fur to thrive upon,
An opportune democracy.

Our silent partner watches from the wings,
Amending covenants long since undone.
He renders beauty from an infant's maiming,
Finds purpose in complete abandon.

I Know an Old Lady

Remember that shopkeeper witnesses named,
passports and cellphones apparently stolen?
He looked like he'd swallowed a fly when informed
Geneva procedure might hurt just a little.
The thing about spiders: you wriggle and jiggle
until they come crawling with pretext for action,
table your issue for further consumption
and leave you encrypted, gibberish data
in parallel networks no bird can divine
or destroy, even with cadenced munitions.
Night vision goggles unclouded by doubt
the cat surveils persons of marginal interest
suspected of nothing but arming the system.
The old lady's fallen and dialed 9-1-1.
Her pit bull roams howling while villagers march,
sickles and pitchforks aloft in the torchlight,
milk cow and carthorse conscripted for meat.
That shopkeeper's next if he doesn't confess.

RENDITION

Surrender does a body good.
Muscles stretched beyond endurance
ease, released from pain's electric shroud,
the minute's respite begged and given,
water soothing arid lips
made loose by prayerful response.
A patient process, this;
to rend soft tissue and extract
one actionable fact,
best exercised where eyes are stone,
ears curl shut like blackened leaves.
A method to elicit
lies where truth will not suffice,
necessary sacrifice of niceties
to learn a name, a date,
a code's enfolded strategies—skins
rendered down to fat.
Ends these days require preemptive means.
Evidence means failure,
post-mortem for events preventable
by questions others will not ask or hazard
answers to, preferring tears
to tactical foreknowledge,

confession to rough countermeasures,
gazing salt-stiff back upon their cities' waste
to arrangements with more permissive states.

JUST CAUSE

A line is crossed, unnoticed by command
But photographed in fame's amoral flash.
Bodies piled, trophy game atop which rests
One boot; smiles of shy surprise, unabashed.

Another line and wilderness surrounds
Us, humid aisles where everything's displayed.
Conscripted to absolve our choices God
Deserts to find a new identity.

We bushwhack through thick scrub, directionless;
The way's degraded, markers overgrown.
Where filthy water swamps the lowest place
We lost crusaders kneel, and choke it down.

SIMULTANEOUS SUBMISSION

One treads lightly before the gods,
Lest too-assertive presence should offend
Fine sensibilities. One bends
Over for inspection, each orifice
Probed for contraband or weapon,
And professes gratitude for such care,
Regret for time consumed, and praise
To ease the terror of their scrutiny.
One's offerings are modest, lines
Descending so to seem innocuous,
Short stairway where a creak unlocks
Encoded ghosts of languages suppressed,
Supposed extinct, last spoken by
That tribe whose rumored artifacts were gleaned
By missionary linguists sent
To civilize rough tongues, so cut them out.
Despite this history, one persists:
Submitting to humiliation's cane,
Accomplice to one's own disgrace,
In the name of principles forgotten
By all but those who died for them
One disregards the written policy
And, with reverence, addresses

Fathers, mothers, beasts or plants, the planets
Cold and bright, one's voice an echo
Stamped returned for insufficient postage.

FRIENDLY FIRE

That dog won't hunt, nor ostrich fly,
that trout won't hasten to the hook.
That staged withdrawal plan's a joke
crusaders whisper while they die.

The rationale's irrational,
mission misallied, delicious
lie from tongues entwined when business
interests coincide. That skull

won't house another soul, which roams
untethered, restlessly between,
cannot ascend, by none redeemed
or mourned, light withering to gloam.

Our maddened hounds have fled to chase
the shades of flightless birds. Undone
we blindly fire into the sun,
that witness prayer won't erase.

WE REGRET TO INFORM YOU

Economies of scale dictate
specific fates, a calculus
where greater good enables one
unhappy outcome at a time
(others' grief negating yours).
We can't account for every life.
Advertising's down, the papers
allocate obituaries
to lives and deaths deemed newsworthy.
The worm's devoured to feed the flock;
objectives require sacrifice,
loss is cross-collateralized
against the term of patient gain,
the upside's ultimate return.
Whoever dies obliges us
to justify with other names
that name beneath the photograph
so no one's left anonymous,
alone in suffering, but shares
the common decencies: a call,
green wreath or funeral bouquet,
official letter of regret
and gratitude for service done—
so many waiting to be mailed

while urgent matters intervene—
condolences expressed above
our signature facsimile.

You Break It, You Bought It

I can't take you anywhere.
Now we own this dangerous
Mistake, combustible beyond repair.
Signs were posted, plain as day:
Do Not Touch Unless You Plan To Purchase.
How many times do I have to say?
Your father will be furious.

Divine advice aside,
What makes you think you own this place?
Maybe your consultant lied,
Amused by earnest plans, and sent
You forth crusading in misguided grace.
Soldiers fall while tidying dissent;
You subsidize the mischief he creates.

So stack the dead in pyramids,
Join mouth to groin, whatever most humiliates.
Engineers and architects grid
Shops where craters yawn, retail paradise
Inviting every human taste.
There nothing is forbidden, no one dies,
And every broken orphan is replaced.

ENDS OR MEANS

Let's not confuse legitimate detention
with what naysayers wrongly christen torture.
Given half the battle's for semantic spoils
we negotiate a win-win protocol,
tweaking witnesses until they lawyer up.
Accords collapse before the blood we signed in
dries, made obsolete by both sides' disregard
for proper usage: infinitives and hairs
split-end through combs of semicolons, repaired
beyond distinguishing facsimile from fact
by experts trained in conflict resolution.
The naked eye can't find the line of fracture.
The naked eye can't see a blessed thing, turned
inside out if necessary to extract
foreknowledge, confirm our worst suspicions are
tomorrow's blindside news. Whatever happens
happens while we sleep, perchance to dream
away the day's intelligence and wake unfettered,
free to go, recalling nothing no-one said.

OCCUPATION

Whatever happens has a purpose now.
Chat emasculates the futures market,
None spared from consequence, the softest breath
Igniting flame that blackens every bough.

Alert but anxious, skeptical though saved,
We're deputized to conquer Babylon.
Each day another headless body found,
Each night exhumes an unattended grave.

Rumors render fear a guilty pleasure;
We're bored with quiet, entertained by threat.
Any chosen citizen's a target,
Prayer offered as preventive measure.

SURGE

Fat lady's victory is sung,
bad apple carameled, then hung

in state to pay the devil's due.
In fullness or the nick of time
the platitudes are pearled anew,

from *Welcome Home* and *Bless This House*
stitched needlepoint on pillowcase

to truth-or-consequences lie
delivered via grip 'n grin,
a threat recast as homily

meant to silence fretful children,
lips zipped to float the zeppelin.

The barn door's barred, bridge burned before
we crossed the t's and dotted i's,
nothing gained from misadventure.

Fooled twice we're not ashamed—sincere
incompetence builds character—

but err again, apologize
for circumstance beyond control,
our unaccounted casualties

borne to ground beneath a tricorn
flag, with which dilemma wipes its horns.

THE HERO

He shifted weight from toe to heel, erect,
rage buttoned down in medaled blues,
meticulous, correct,
observing our authority. Refused

the chair left free by everyone,
heard levelly all latecomers' respects,
surrounded but alone.
We gobbled sandwiches and antidotal juice,

our noncombatant share of spoils,
roast beef glistening on teeth.
His eyes were terrible.
He'd come to front a writer's pitch, beneath

contempt: a book, adrenal rush
for spectators and open casket for the souls
of friends he'd lost. Voice hushed,
professionally wreathed

with tact long practice brings, his ghost began:
Dug into a fogbound ridge
above a village in Afghanistan,
his SEALs surveyed the video mirage,

their highest valued head,
who walked in white among his clan,
inviting snipers, unafraid,
his martyrdom our privilege.

Then bells invaded their redoubt.
Bearded elders gazed at them, absurd,
chewing gravely, lost in thought,
goatherds shouting foreign words

the team mistook for praise,
so offered cigarettes. The ambush caught
them from behind, amazed,
blind with blood and mortared

deaf, razed by enfilade.
The last alive, legs shot to shit,
face torn half-off by hand grenade
he killed five terrorists,

furtive men with skinning knives
who hunted him and paid
for getting close, their lives
his to resurrect in nightly visits.

Eyes askance, the hero winced.
His writer paused to bask in self-regard.
Orchestrating silence
he measured our diminishment, prepared:

Ya'll think this book is worth your while?
Will it please your audience?
Your kids are next, it's all a dress rehearsal
now. Aghast, we stared

each other down, lunchmeat stiffening, curled dry,
unable to believe the obvious,
as if a witness to Thermopylae
brought news too true to trust—

the banquet hall in disarray,
our not-for-attribution lies
confessed, armies swept away
like table scrapes before a god's disgust.

DENIABILITY

A leak implies without affirming fact;
there's wiggle room should details contradict,
events reverse themselves, a photograph
prove forged. Whose grasp of evidence is firm
enough to verify its chain, each link
unblemished by the bottom muck of time?
Consider your child's birth certificate,
Mom's recipes, amendments to your will—
if you've lost these then how's intelligence
know missile shed from shadow, extract sense
from cellphone intercepts where coded threat's
expressed as wedding plans? Network anchors
bargain ratings higher, negotiate
for access to exclusive video.

Officials fashion lullaby from lie,
commitment into exit strategy
conveyed in semaphore, averted eyes
a silent language undercutting words.
Truth's relative as beauty, circumstance
our ever-shifting standard, as an urn's
exhumed pastoral darkens to reveal
a priest receiving sacrificial girls
with oil and fire, their moistened limbs consigned

to greater good, the glaze that purifies.
You turn it, passerby, obliged to none,
witness without testimony, faint sough
of bone and ash inside this artifact
the only evidence you can't deny.

III

TURN

A glint prefigures it, red
mote igniting in the eye's
July. Can't be blinked away,
wept green again; irritant,
shard—leaf scarlet at the edge,
blemish on a healthy cheek—
it takes root comfortably
beside a duct. Out of sight,
out of mind, an optimist
opines, until the next leaf
turns, is recognized as lens
through which to view its forebear.
Then, too late, the tears begin.

Our days grow short, evenings cool.
Hawks patrol the roads for kills.
The hills are flame, the lake rim
fringed by fallen leaves and fronds,
and one by one our homes fall
dark, like lamps left on a time.
Barren fields are touched with rime.

THE THIRD PIG

Anyone can smell it coming,
rank meaty breath and ticking claws.
Hindsight so enhanced prescience
you apprehend the end before
due credit's claimed or blame assigned
to splinter groups as yet unnamed.
Warned, you make escape provisions,
hoard water and electric tape,
surf uninterrupted broadcasts,
test batteries and buy a gun.
Car alarm crescendos summon
first responders, rotors hammer
telegraphic reassurance—
got it got it got it got it—
but something's up, the anchorman
makes signal codes of frowns and grins
that contradict his scripted news,
agenda none but you discerns.
Each day's a cautionary tale
you listen to, a child again,
mesmerized by Dad exclaiming
Wolf! to villagers once-bitten
into doubt, Chicken Little's squawks
against the imminent collapse,

the mine canary whistling one
inquiring note into the dark,
then pausing to inhale, and wait.

A SUDDEN LOSS OF CABIN PRESSURE

My seatcushion's a flotation device.
We're vouchsafed the buckle's operation.
Should our captain take evasive action
a mask will lower bearing oxygen,
the exit aisle undulate with lights.

Doubt is the mother of engineering,
each *what if* answered patiently by *then*.
Aloft, free to move about the cabin,
I lose the lingo's swagger, imagine
engine trouble, fuel tank sparks, wind shearing

from above, inhuman shove our bowels
cower from and loosen in submission,
which is praise. Severe attendants listen,
minister to special dispensation,
collect our trash and offer moistened towels'

ablution, drinks before descent's begun.
The captain drones ground temperature and time,
illuminates the fasten seat belt sign,
then dims the plane, voice harsh through static grind,
wishing well on behalf of everyone,

whatever our final destination.

PERSON OF INTEREST

We're looking for whoever didn't board,
some face surveillance failed to match against
its database, an unknown alias,
drifter handymen driving stolen vans.
No one's suspect; we're ruling people out.
Your call remains anonymous unless
arrest begets conviction and reward—
you'll be coming forward to collect, yes?
We're working leads, questioning the neighbors
(unmarried men with meticulous yards),
hold details close to filter wannabes
from players, who might barter names for time.
(The pro-life laid-off middle manager.)
Liberty's measured by the tangible:
licenses and passports, identi-kits
where teeth and childhood fractures correlate,
stray facts the Web collects like flies or dew,
cookies, emails, consumer vapor trails
(priests who download monuments and blueprints)—
receipts of daily life a hologram
we recognize in glimpses, as if strobed,
revealed by interims of light, then gone.
We only want what's best for everyone.

Will you accept the blame if God forbid--?
We're looking, but it's out of hand when kids'
imaginary friends are terrorists.
(Whoever moves their lips while reading this.)

TEST

In the event of an emergency
official information is dispensed
via broadcast systems, tests of which

have interrupted programming these years
at untimely moments—a siren switch-
blade cutting off romantic song mid-verse

to ruin your maneuver for a kiss,
the tv's companionable murmurs
jerked taut by threat, seemingly prophetic:

A test, this is only a test.
Please do not call authorities.
Groundless speculation fosters panic.

Okay. You wait it out, channel changer
steady as a gun. The movie of the week
resumes: some blind woman in a wheelchair

skirts grave danger, though she doesn't know it
yet. You wonder if the information's
fresh or stale, bread or hardened crust left

over, table wine or real thing whelming
fragile glassware, the nervous spokesman
choking on the blood, the blood, the genuine?

Suspicious Acts

Aware of being watched, Suspicious
goes about his business,
brushes, showers, shaves, and dresses
in the dark, impeccably innocuous.
Explaining nothing (nothing to explain),
the picture of responsible routine
bequeaths his wife a note: *Burn this.*
Gun to head you wouldn't notice
anything amiss, striding for the train,
alert, deliberate, contained.
A knowing wink, conspiratorial,
gives technicians something to surveil,
enlarge and slow, freeze-frame analyze,
explode to pixels, recomprise.
Shoulders back, chin patrician,
Suspicious disregards the posted signs
and loiters like a criminal,
train after train's departure and arrival
bearing hives of nervous drones
who glimpse him, smiling but alone,
perhaps with foreknowledge
only trained interrogators dredge
in nations where their craft's permissible.
Cigarette as prop, a movie still,

he lets the trains' wakes roar around him,
accidental seraphim,
whirling leaves and dust a cloak in which
Suspicious all but vanishes—
a breath drawn deep,
an ember's livid tip
aglow with revelation—

                 gone.

HIDE AND SEEK

Enough of hollow protocol.
Persuaded by intelligence
surmised from noise the system's culled
through parallel surveillances,

we know it's so that we don't know.
Does God reveal himself or hide?
Satellites peer into shadows.
Decision, or the mushroom cloud?

Bureaucracies contend, align
surprise while pause seems possible—
squirrels vanish, birds recombine
with leaves' pale undersides—until

a predatory drone surrounds
our darkened town and something ripped
to pieces screams, then quiets down.
Heaven, or what we've made of it.

PAGING

In hospitals and airports, places where
arrival or departure
collect us, one is called,
the intercom invades most private nooks—
graffitied restroom stall, a chapel's
narrow pew of whisperers.
Though ours is not the name announced
we look up curious from books,
hush children still, tilt ears toward ceiling grates
where the speaker's secreted,
though its voice sounds everywhere. We wait.

A woman stands, maybe just awakened,
tucking clothes in place and smoothing rumpled hair,
to approach the information desk or lift
the red-lit courtesy phone.
From our vantages we stare,
point out and crane for better view
of one who receives news beyond
our strength to bear if we could hear,
yet takes it calm, eyes cast down
but bright, as if she knew
the story's end, beginning now.

NIGHTMARE SCENARIO

Give the public what they fear, without which
Pendant blade above collective necks
We mute the voice with nothing to predict.
No future in maintaining status quo.
Our seers vie for eyeballs, clicking through
Scenarios of escalating hex:
An infant suffocates, a forest falls,
The sun exhales its bleary morning pall
And elevates the seas, their weed-thick shroud
Compressing us to souls or fossilized
Remains, depends which god you recognize.

Meanwhile breakfast's done, children kiss goodbye
And wave. A day like any other save
The one you've made provisions to survive,
Rehearsed escape and stockpiled core supplies,
When immanence surrounds the skins of things,
As if each body passing by eclipsed
The herald star—immense, descending ring—
So glow and shadow join in time's ellipse,
A dance until whatever happens next.

PAY NO ATTENTION TO THAT MAN BEHIND THE CURTAIN

A little blood to whet the appetite.
A stob, ignited to unman
Our flammable elite
Who quail and pray for rain, a brazen head
Commanding supplicants to bow.
We've stripped the witch and shipped her last effects
To relatives that disavow
All knowledge and renounce her debts.
The kingdom's our dominion now,
Impossible to leave, the great balloon—
Umbilicals cut free—
Ascends uncaptained through blue sky,
Defying no-fly zones
Above the ruling classes' summer homes.
A curtain pulled by accident
Reveals machines, amplifying
Sly lies we thought divine,
The bait-and-switch a covenant
Contrived to buy its maker time to flee,
Scuttering for parts unknown. Our slippers
Click like lighters low on fuel:
A farm adrift in mist
Emerges in the mind as if entranced,
Furrows scythed to stalks and cellar

Casketed with fruit, the princess
Sleeping off concussion,
Her dream an undisclosed locale
No map will name and none confess
Unless she's kissed
Awake, to tell us of a place
We recognize, but can't quite face.

IF YOU SEE SOMETHING, SAY SOMETHING

Not understanding why
Suspicious kneels, ashamed
by faith's default cliché,
unsettled by surprise
too great to improvise
against. So clenches eyes,
a child beside the bed
his desk's become, to see
not God (to which each day's
decapitated dead
appealed without avail),
but lesser entities,
victims of circumstance
beyond control, devil
unforeseen in details
some expert didn't sweat,
walls breached by viral spam.
He genuflects in case
observance matters: cross
inscribed on chest, salaam
six ways from Sunday—check,
smudge brow with ashtray grit,
bow, cup hands, meditate
on Yahweh, Buddha, Zeus,

Anubis, Loki, L.
Ron Hubbard's frozen head....
Suspicious stagger steps
erect, breathing ragged
as if pursued but fled,
patient adversary
persuading weaker prey
who pause to listen, rapt
by glottal chittering—
something blah blah something—
a tongue, an alphabet's
transliterated code,
street name they'd kill to know.

TRIDENT

We rush to justify the practiced lie
when excrement disables hindsight's eye,
this ceasefire fails, that exit strategy's

postponed. Extenuating circumstance
prevails against best practices and plans,
Excel and Powerpoint undone by chance

encounters, infectious viral blisters.
While we're vacationing one wingbeat stirs
a tropical disturbance, disinters

the restless natives' shallow self-dug graves—
denied, erased, all but forgotten save
one inconvenient photograph, conveyed

by satellite to screens we're rapt before,
rubbernecking witnesses to terror,
the genuine reduced to metaphor.

Information drifts in radiant shards,
pixeled images, interrupted words.
Our midnight doubtful alibis are heard

as prayer, euphemisms crunched like sweets
by teeth impatient for the core's release.
Give us this day our daily dead police,

our mortared mosque, our rape, the usual.
Record the damage as collateral
against our leveraged power to enthrall.

WATCH LIST

Each night's color coded panic level,
each spike of chatter the authorities
deem meaningful becomes less real, a cry
we villagers ignore, too often warned.
It isn't news unless it entertains
or terrifies, depending on your taste.
Dead stowaways, unattended baggage,
the child whose name alarms intelligence,
rehearsals of disaster and response,
finger whorls preserved, photos digitized
against the day, the grounded planes, the piers'
enchanted wood of cranes made silhouette
by searchlight....
                    On our block the watchers kiss
blue liquid screens goodnight, draw shades, dim lights
except for one: the porch, to welcome home
late children or repel a stranger guest,
through which from which cannot be distinguished.

NINE-TENTHS OF THE LAW

Snafu futurists concur
it isn't if but when we're
overtaken by events
that render fallback systems
obsolete, a cluster-fuck
no code can disentangle.
Boys and girls it's never now,
shirts against skins, run or gun,
a raise for anyone who
chisels fire from flint to sticks.
We can't go back; it isn't
what it was, the mind's-eye map's
undone, eminent domain
made streets canals and cratered
old-growth trees. Who remembers
who or where our parents were?
Our names are theirs diminished,
echoes fading over—out.
We follow fossil footsteps
nowhere in particular,
then wander downtown asking
passersby directions home.
Careful faces turn away,
studious in disregard

for history, having seized
the days from open schedules,
synchronized their clocks awry,
forged our signatures to wills
and dispossessed our heirs by
failing to record the deed.

No Brainer

Civil war this, civil war that.
It's murder playing tit for tat,
no time to cull and dress our dead
before fresh chum arrives on ice.

The disembodied head's rapt eyes
behold the lens we focus through,
suspense orchestrally induced,
thumbs poised to channel click when bored.

We don't condone, but redefine;
outsource unpleasantness to friends.
One man's torture is another's
healing touch, glass half-empty filled

until breath bursts in mother tongue
extinct since cooler heads prevailed,
false witness rendered genuine
by professional immersion.

FAILURE TO COMPLY

Seduced by legalese
we undress piece by piece

belts and suits penitential shoes
inspectors wand us through

surrender laptops cellphones keys
to mortgaged kingdoms property's

our status quo and credit line
complicit citizens

except that woman's squalling flock
with any luck they're screwed Ziploc

insufficiently transparent
we wink in mutual assent

guess she didn't get the memo
what goes for us means you

eye level screen restrictions scroll
no scissors fluids alcohol's

allowed if duty free
one nation under penalty

of law look who's going postal
I'll give you something to surveil

she slings the diaper bag
unwadded contents hemorrhage

goldfish wipes cartoon brand pull-ups
suspicious sippy cup

my god what garbage cops converge
around the demiurge

one bends to confiscate it spoils
of war her baby wails

Motherfuckers eyes wild
she's doubled over down and held

arms bent behind her cuffed
okay enough's enough

we back away say nothing no
one notices us go

Likenesses

The specialist displayed his handiwork:
before and after photographs of kids
disfigured by genetic quirk—
ears clenched buds, noses incomplete—fitted
with prosthetics. He'd designed disguises
for CIA-led foreign escapades,
transfigured diplomats and spies
who fled their veils, identities unmade.
His pages turned to war's portfolio,
the burned, bombed, slashed to ribbons, branded, shot,
someone's children made to swallow
our proclivities, merciful or not.
"So much of who we are," he said, "depends
on markers humans recognize as us."
I recalled our daughter Helen
shying from my stroke-strange mother's kisses,
two years enough to discern alien
in familiar guise. Random casualties
of fragile chromosome or gun,
invention or divine efficiency,
can children fathom what we have in mind—
reconstructed in our broken image,
comforting likenesses, our kind,
ours to crush again and mend the damage?

SOFT TARGETS

Everything's amiss: the briefcase
Time forgot, documents erased,
Suspicious mail, malingerers
Giving cameras the finger.
The CIA director prays;
Our President's on holiday.
The news conveys scenarios
Rehearsed by impresarios
Of fear; we watch them entertain,
Enrapt by images of pain
Not ours, but others' to endure.
Vigilance makes us insecure,
Unnerved by fellow citizens
Surveilling us. I listen in
On cellphone arguments and read
My seatmate's laptop email screed
Against her boss; my hooded eyes
Feign sleep, a patriotic spy's.

We pass through towns to meadowlands:
Miles of reedy marsh, abandoned
Highway trestle going nowhere,
Quonset hut and boarded-over
Cinderblock a polar outpost

Inhabited by fog or ghost.
One heron stalks its blackened pond.
The shadow city flickers on,
Horizon dark—no guarantees.
Each day unsettles certainty.
We're told to shop, buy homes, invest,
Our capital divinely blessed,
Then quail whenever power fails.
Authority's provisional;
Obituaries of Marines—
Assured, invincible, nineteen—
Make trivial our politics,
Our well-fed appetite for tricks
That blind and gag the populace.
Whatever plan our god creates
Cannot undo the human flame
Of faiths igniting in his name.
These meadowlands will burn and rise
Without us, barren paradise
Where stadiums such worship built
Erode from monuments to silt.

Our train arrives in Hoboken
Intact, nothing bombed or broken.
The loudspeaker's imperious—
Remove your personal effects—
As if we'll be identified

Post-true-believer's-suicide
By newspaper and coffee cup,
Ticket, backpack, comb and makeup,
Wallet photographs of children.
My daughter's voice beneath the din
Pipes up, unbidden as a bird's,
Her absence present in each word,
Like air where motes in sunlight glow
Alone, recombine as shadow.
Where are we going? I don't know;
Someplace safe where none will follow.
Who will be waiting? Everyone
From home is gone, we're on our own.
Why? I can't explain, there isn't
Time. Don't worry, honey: listen—